Spiritual
Understanding
& Prayer

SUP

on a Stand Up
Paddleboard

By Lori Bumgarner

Foreword by Candice Appleby,
champion SUP racer and pro surfer

SUP:
Spiritual Understanding & Prayer on a Stand Up Paddleboard

Copyright © 2017, by Lori Bumgarner
ISBN: 978-0-9990090-0-0

Foreword: Candice Appleby
Editors: Jessa Rose Sexton &
Rosemary J. Hilliard
Cover and Book Design: Whitnee Clinard

Published by Hilliard Press

Franklin, Tennessee
Oxford, England

www.hilliardinstitute.com

Spiritual Understanding & Prayer

SUP

on a Stand Up Paddleboard

By Lori Bumgarner

Foreword by Candice Appleby,
champion SUP racer and pro surfer

HILLIARD
PRESS

Acknowledgements

My Lord and Savior Jesus Christ, Tracy
Larkin, Ryan and Cristy Mayes, Sarah
Perrotto, Katie Gooch, Neil Newton,
Cindy Sorci, Jessa R. Sexton, K. Mark
Hilliard, Rosemary J. Hilliard, Whitnee
Clinard, Veronica Franks, Candice
Appleby, and members of the Nashville
and Brentwood chapters of Fellowship of
Companies for Christ International

TABLE OF CONTENTS

FOREWORD

INTRODUCTION

BEGINNINGS

GROWTH

MOMENTUM

CONCLUSION

ABOUT THE AUTHOR

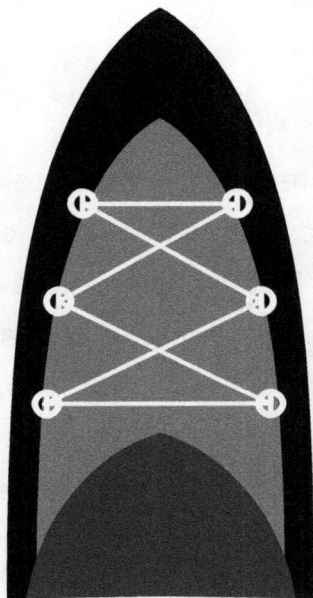

FOREWORD

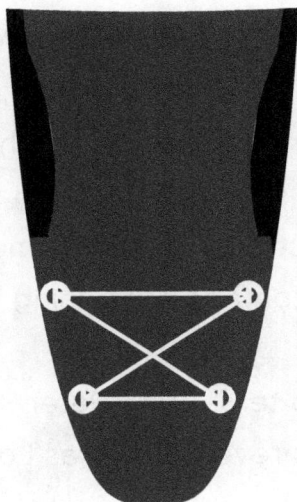

I'm so excited and honored to introduce to you a devotional that hits very close to home, but first I want to share a bit about the author. Lori Bumgarner is a woman of passion. She's an outdoor lover and avid stand up paddler who encourages others as a certified life and transformational coach. With a degree in psychology and education, Lori is the owner of paNASH, a passion and career coaching service.

Above all, Lori's greatest passion is her love for Christ and dedication to sharing His Word. In the pages of this devotional, Lori shares stories of courage, strength, hope, and much more through her adventures in stand up paddling from the beginning stages as a first timer, to being the instructor, and everything in between.

God's word tells us in 1 Peter 3:15, "But in your hearts revere Christ as Lord. Always

be prepared to give an answer to everyone who asks you to give the reason for
the hope that you have. But do this with
gentleness and respect" (NIV).

Through her adventures on a SUP board,
Lori does just that. With beautifully apt
biblical comparisons and real encounters
of grace, *SUP: Spiritual Understanding
and Prayer on a Stand Up Paddleboard*
is a great source of encouragement for
those who are trying something new,
who are reaching for a goal, or who
simply desire to learn more about God's
goodness and the power of prayer.

As a follower of Jesus and a professional
stand up paddler, I find this book to be
a great resource of daily inspiration and
hope. The first chapter takes me right
back to my early days as a beginner, and
also reminds me of how quickly things

can change when I take my eyes off Jesus. There was a time in my SUP racing career where my spiritual vision grew blurry, and although I knew God gifted me for His glory, I was finding my worth in worldly victories that couldn't last. It took a season of growth, and ultimately injury, to help me realize that I couldn't put my identity in something that could be taken from me.

> *Don't you realize that in a race everyone runs, but only one person gets the prize? So run to win! All athletes are disciplined in their training. They do it to win a prize that will fade away, but we do it for an eternal prize. So I run with purpose in every step. I am not just shadowboxing. I discipline my body like an athlete, training it to do what it should. Otherwise, I fear that after*

preaching to others I myself might be
disqualified.
(1 Corinthians 9:24-27 NLT)

In that season of injury, I was met ever-more by God's goodness and His ability to work all things together for good, for those who love Him and who are called according to His purpose (Romans 8:28). I now know that SUP is the lampstand God has gifted me with to shine His light for His Glory, and that my identity is secure when it is in Him. Lori knows this truth, and she shares it beautifully in the coming pages.

It is my prayer for all of you who read this book that the truth of God's good-ness penetrates your heart and that, through Lori's adventures in SUP and God's Word, you find strength to run the race that God has marked for you with

more hope and assurance than ever before.

Candice Appleby
champion SUP racer and pro surfer

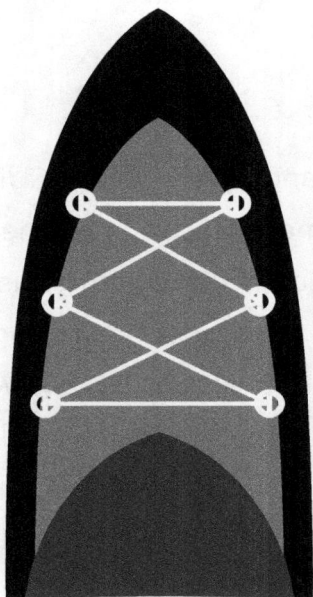

INTRODUCTION

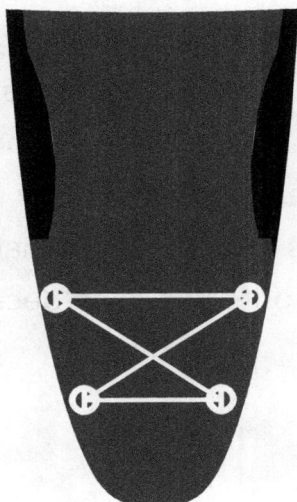

I began stand up paddling (SUP) in the early summer of 2014 at a time when I was questioning where my business and my career were headed. Though feeling a little burned out on my work as an image consultant in the music industry, I was afraid to let go of the business I'd spent nearly seven years building. I was constantly trying to figure out what God wanted me to do next.

Since I wasn't getting an answer right away like I had hoped, I just kept praying and kept plugging along in my business while also taking some classes on things that interested me and learning some new hobbies: like SUP. Out of all the new things I was trying recreationally, SUP was my favorite and soon became a passion.

Unlike my regular morning prayer and devotion time, paddling provided a quiet place away from my day-to-day environment to truly hear from God. The serenity out on the water and away from everything else was just what I needed. While I didn't get an immediate answer to my prayers regarding my career, I was constantly reminded of God's Word each time I was out on the water.

SUP: Spiritual Understanding & Prayer

As soon as I recognized the parallels between God's Word and what I was learning as a beginning paddler, I felt an urge to write. So, I started a blog called "SUP: Spiritual Understanding & Prayer on a SUP." The blog wasn't something I heavily promoted; I shared it with only a few friends and trusted God that it would reach whomever He wanted it to reach.

One of those friends I shared my blog with was another woman my age I'd met that summer. She had started paddling around the same time I did. Some days we'd paddle together and talk about our walk with God. It turned out she was having some similar struggles regarding her own career. We promised to stay in prayer for each other.

That first year I paddled every month of the year, even in the dead of the Tennessee winter. The days when there were reasonable temperatures and sunny skies in January and February were rare, but I took advantage and got out on my board when I could. Doing so gave me more to write about in my blog.

Still No Answer

When summer 2015 rolled around, I was still feeling restless in my career, and I was having the worst year of my business I'd had since I first started it after leaving my previous job as a career adviser. I know what you're thinking, "How could someone who used to be a career adviser not know what she wants to be when she grows up?" Well, I did know, and I had pursued it, and now I didn't know what was next. But I kept praying and kept trusting that, in His time, God would reveal His purpose for me in this season of my life.

I'd become so passionate about stand up paddling that I considered how I could possibly do some type of work in that field: something besides opening my own shop. I spent the summer of 2015 kicking around the idea of doing some kind of group or corporate training using SUP. After all, I did have past experience of teaching and training, and teaching is one of my spiritual gifts. Also at that point I already had experience teaching the SUP 101 class at my local shop. But my idea never seemed to formulate into a deliverable. That is, not until the week of my birthday.

Learning to Listen to the Holy Spirit

On December 15, 2015, I went to my local SUP shop. I'd bought my first board there shortly after learning to paddle. The plan was to trade in my current 12'6" race board for a 14' race board. It was an unusually warm winter day in the 70s, so

I was able to get out on the water and test drive some 14-footers. But, I just did not have a good feeling in my gut about the board I had been so sure I wanted.

I knew the new board would cost more than my current board, and there was no guarantee the shop owner would be able to sell my current board to help pay for the new one, but that wasn't what caused my hesitation. The problem was, every time I got on the 14' board, it didn't sit well with my soul. It also didn't seem to fit me physically. I was too light for a board that size, and I didn't feel as comfortable on it as I did on the board that had served me so well for the past year and a half.

I decided to listen to my gut and not make any decisions that day. I left there a little disappointed, but knew I needed to spend some time praying. After all, I'd prayed about the first board, and it turned out to be a wise purchase. Since it was my birthday, and I was driving by a Cracker Barrel restaurant on my way home, I decided to stop in for some of their Coca-Cola cake as a treat to myself for turning 42.

As I was waiting for my dessert, I prayed about the unsettling feeling I was having about the new board. Then, I checked my email on my phone and happened to see a promotional message from the SUP shop for a sale on inflatable boards. I almost deleted the email because I wasn't interested, or so I thought. Instead, I decided to open the message and began reading.

As I read, I realized that an inflatable board made much more sense than a

new race board because, at the sale price, I could keep my current board and therefore have two. Not only that, when an inflatable is deflated, it could be rolled up and thrown in the trunk of my car, making for easy transportation. Since I had to replace my car earlier that year, I no longer had a vehicle with a rack on it and would have had to spend extra money on a car rack in order to transport a larger race board. An inflatable board would affordably solve that problem and would make traveling with it easier!

The best reason for an inflatable board is, since they are great for beginners, I knew I could take friends out on it! Having two boards would allow me to share my passion with others, teach them how to paddle, and even tell them more about my blog to spread God's Word. I immediately called the SUP owner and said, "Nix the 14-footer. I want the inflatable you have for sale!" My gut, which was really the Holy Spirit, told me that was the way to go. There were no feelings of hesitation on that decision at all.

God Doesn't Waste Anything

Two days after my birthday and after I ordered the inflatable SUP, I finally got an answer to my year and a half long prayer about my career. God made it so clear that I had a vision of the answer as if it appeared in a flashing neon sign. The answer was PASSION. I suddenly realized I needed to use my past experience as a career adviser and my thirst for developing new passions of my own to help others find ways to incorporate passion into their own careers and lives.

I'd be using my number one spiritual gift of encouragement, along with my other spiritual gift of teaching, to show people how to use job search skills and lifelong learning as a launching pad to a life and career that uses their gifts and passions, resulting in purpose and joy.

Just to show how God doesn't waste anything, all the skills I had developed running my own image consulting company would be used in running my own career coaching practice. The career coaching skills weren't going to waste either. God showed me how to repackage them in a more meaningful way by incorporating a focus on passion. In fact, I even got to keep the same name for my career coaching practice as I had for my image consulting business. It still fit perfectly even though my mission had changed.

SUP: SPIRITUAL UNDERSTANDING & PRAYER

And the best part is I'm now even incorporating stand up paddling in my work with my career coaching clients. SUP not only has spiritual parallels but also parallels to life and work. I've been able to take clients out on my inflatable board and not only show them those parallels, but also provide them a different environment to think about their current situation, resulting in a different perspective.

One client commented on how rejuvenating the experience was for her mind, not just her body. Another client said the experience brought her back to basics and back to a time when she used to be on the crew team in college. SUP was a reminder to her of what she'd always had a desire to pursue professionally and now had the confidence to do so.

God Speaks through
Your Passions

Although it took a year and a half before I got the answer to my prayer, I continued to seek understanding and remained patient. I kept praying, both for me and for my friend, who, by the way, also discovered the next step in her career shortly after I did.

While your interest may be something totally different from my love of SUP, I pray that, as you read this devotional book, you'll be able to see God's Word reflected in your own passions and pursuits. Don't just listen to Him when you're reading your Bible and praying, but also when you're working and playing. He's still speaking even then.

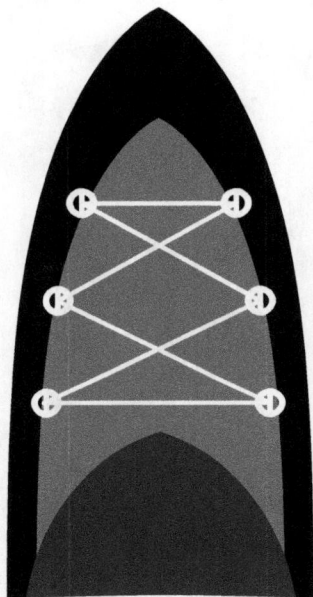

BEGINNINGS

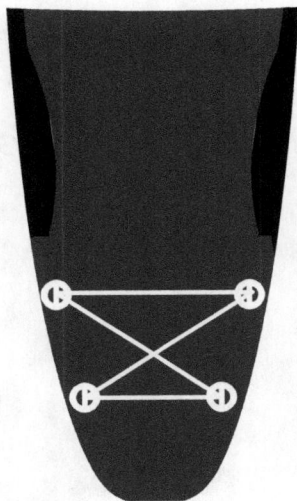

DAY 1:

Don't Look Down

But when he looked down at the waves
churning beneath his feet, he lost his
nerve and started to sink. He cried,
"Master, save me!"
(Matthew 14:30 MSG)

After first seeing and hearing about stand up paddle boarding (SUP), I decided I was going to try it, but not on the ocean. I wanted to try it first on flat water, and figured there had to be a place near me here in Nashville since we have a large river and several lakes.

After a quick search online, I found a place at the marina closest to me that rents boards and offers a beginner course, making the thought of trying this new sport a little less intimidating. I invited a few friends to join me, but didn't have any takers. I didn't let the fact that I'd have to go solo stop me. I've been to the other side of the world to Australia by myself. I go hiking and biking by myself all the time. I could do this by myself too. And besides, I knew I wouldn't be truly alone because God is always with me, and there would be some other newbies in the beginner class I could meet.

Not personally knowing anyone who had previously tried SUP, I wasn't sure if it was going to be harder than it looked or easier than it looked. Would I have the balance to get up and stay up on the first try? I mean, you're basically standing on water! I was sure it was something that probably doesn't come naturally, at least not at first.

Despite how hot it was that day, I didn't want to end up swimming with turtles in the Cumberland River if I could help it. So before heading out to the marina I prayed, "Lord, please let me be able to get up on the board on the first try and stay standing up." (It's true you can pray anytime about anything!)

Not only did God answer that prayer, but throughout the process of the beginner's lesson, He showed me just how much this experience of learning SUP is a direct parallel to some of the lessons in His Word. For instance, just as I was about to stand up for the first time, the instructor told me to keep my focus on the horizon and not look down or I would likely fall in the water. As soon as she said that, I immediately thought of the story of Peter when he walked on water with Jesus:

> *As soon as the meal was finished, he insisted that the disciples get in the boat and go on ahead to the other side while he dismissed the people. With the crowd dispersed, he climbed the mountain so he could be by himself and pray. He stayed there alone, late into the night.*

Meanwhile, the boat was far out to sea when the wind came up against them and they were battered by the waves. At about four o'clock in the morning, Jesus came toward them walking on the water. They were scared out of their wits. "A ghost!" they said, crying out in terror.

But Jesus was quick to comfort them. "Courage, it's me. Don't be afraid."

Peter, suddenly bold, said, "Master, if it's really you, call me to come to you on the water."

*He said, "Come ahead." Jumping out of the boat, Peter walked on the water to Jesus. **But when he looked down at the waves churning beneath his feet, he lost his nerve and started to sink. He cried, "Master, save me!"***

Immediately Jesus reached out his hand and caught him. "You of little faith," he said, "why did you doubt?"

And when they climbed into the boat, the wind died down. Then those who were in the boat worshiped him, saying, "Truly you are the Son of God." (Matthew 14:22-30 MSG, 31-33 NIV) emphasis added

Peter started to sink because he took his focus off Jesus.

One of the other things the instructor told us was, "Your board will go where your eyes go." This is why it is so important for us to guard what we look at and watch. If we take our focus off of God and peer down the path of darkness and destruction, before we know it we're likely to be steering ourselves in that direction and heading down that road.

Take time like Jesus did to be by yourself and pray. Be like Peter and take a step in faith. Don't look down. Keep your eyes on God, and when you feel like you're sinking, reach out for Jesus's loving hand. He will catch you.

DAY 2:
My Brain on SUP – Staying focused on what's deep, not what's shallow

What a miracle of skin and bone, muscle and brain! You gave me life itself, and incredible love. You watched and guarded every breath I took.
(Job 10:11-12 MSG)

After my first time stand up paddle boarding, I couldn't wait to get back out on the water. The next time I went, I took my friend Veronica who was a little nervous at first just like I was, but took to it very easily. Come to find out, she was experienced in snow and water skiing, so she really had nothing to be worried about.

While we were in the harbor about to go onto the river, I saw a few turtles swimming around, and then I noticed something in the water that at first I thought was just a plastic bag. When I looked closer, it appeared to be either a jellyfish or even a brain! Well, I knew it couldn't be a jellyfish since we were paddling in fresh water, and I was really hoping it wasn't a brain!

I asked the co-owner of the SUP shop what it was. She said it was a bryozoan, a rare thing to see. (She must be right because I haven't seen one again in over two years of paddling.) A bryozoan is a colony of tiny animals that form jelly-like masses and filter particles from the water. I continue to be amazed by God's creation!

After we got out of the harbor, there's a little section you have to go through to get onto the river that is rather shallow on one side. The co-owner reminded me not to get too close to the shallow edge because I could run aground and take a hard fall. I wasn't too worried about falling because, just like last time, I prayed for God to keep me on the board, and I was really starting to get into a groove with paddling this second time around.

But I still appreciated the advice and heeded the warning.

I also considered this advice in terms of my spiritual life, and remembered how, when I'm not spending time deep in the Word of God, I tend to focus on shallow things which can really throw my sense of peace off balance and off course. That's why I have to spend time every morning digging deep into the Word before I do anything else, not just to feed my brain spiritually, but also to filter out all the impure particles of messages from culture and the media that daily bombard my mind. I can always tell the difference in my sense of peace if I miss a day of God's Word, and therefore try not to do so. I encourage you also to make a habit of feeding your brain daily with a healthy portion of God's Word!

In my first two times of paddle boarding, I discovered just how peaceful SUP is. When I'm out on the water, I don't think about anything negative. All my worries and concerns melt away, much like when I'm spending time in the Word. This is one reason why SUP has become a regular part of my life.

DAY 3:
Stand Your Ground
and
Face the Waves

Finally, be strong in the Lord and in his mighty power. Put on the full armor of God, so that you can take your stand against the devil's schemes.
(Ephesians 6:10, 11 NIV)

The first time I went out to paddle by myself, it was kind of a last minute decision because it had been raining that morning and looked like it would continue throughout the day. But once the sun came shining through in late afternoon, I couldn't stay inside much longer. I thought about going for a bike ride, but opted instead for a paddle because I had become so hooked! So, I hopped online to reserve a board and then headed over to the marina.

This time I went out later in the day when there are more boats out, making the water a little more choppy. I actually like it when the boats create wake because it's kind of cool to feel the board rocking under my feet and to be challenged to stay standing on the board in the waves. I remembered what I was taught in the beginner class: when the waves come, turn your board toward them and face them.

God doesn't promise us a trouble-free life with smooth sailing. Instead, there will be times of trials (John 16:33), but Jesus' presence gives us the peace to face those trials. We can put on the Armor of God in order to stand against evil:

> *Finally, be strong in the Lord and in his mighty power. Put on the full armor of God, so that you can take your stand against the devil's schemes. For our struggle is not against flesh and blood, but against the rulers, against the authorities, against the powers of this dark world and against the spiritual forces of evil in the heavenly realms. Therefore put on the full armor of God, so that when the day of evil comes, you may be able to stand your ground, and*

after you have done everything, to stand. Stand firm then, with the belt of truth buckled around your waist, and the body armor of God's righteousness. For shoes, put on the peace that comes from the Good News so that you will be fully prepared. In addition to all of these, hold up the shield of faith to stop the fiery arrows of the devil. Put on salvation as your helmet, and take the sword of the Spirit, which is the word of God. Pray in the Spirit at all times and on every occasion. Stay alert and be persistent in your prayers for all believers everywhere.
(Ephesians 6:10-14 NIV; 15-18 NLT)

The passage above came to mind when I was thinking about the gear required for SUP. Maybe this is a bit of a stretch, but I see parallels here:

SUP: SPIRITUAL UNDERSTANDING & PRAYER

- Belt pack life jacket :: belt of truth
  - ° If you fall off your board, the personal floatation device (PFD) is your first protection against drowning. In the same vein, God's truth keeps us from drowning in despair. And His truth keeps us afloat when darkness and doubt swirl around us like angry waves.

- Board :: body armor of God's righteousness
  - ° The board is obviously the most important piece for stand up paddling, allowing you to stand steady and upright on top of the water. *The righteousness of the blameless will direct his way aright, but the wicked will fall by his own wickedness. The righteousness of the upright will*

deliver them, but the unfaithful
will be caught by their lust
(Proverbs 11:4-6 NKJV).

- Ankle leash :: shoes of peace
  - ° The ankle leash is your second defense from drowning. When you're wearing a leash, nothing can separate you from your board if you fall off of it. Even when we fall in our walk with God, nothing, neither height nor depth, can separate us from God's love in Christ Jesus (Romans 8:39).

- Sunscreen :: shield of faith
  - ° Sunscreen is an important and powerful tool. It shields us from the dangers of the sun and provides a coating of safety. Faith does the same thing in our daily

walk. It protects us from exposure to all kinds of danger.

- Hat/visor :: helmet of salvation
  - ° Wearing a hat or visor while paddling protects not only your head but also your vision, which is beyond value in this sport. Keeping your sight on Jesus (Hebrews 12:2) is the only way to survive the trials of life, knowing there is better to come.

- Paddle :: sword of the Spirit; the Word of God
  - ° The paddle is the only piece of equipment that is used both defensively and offensively. Just like the sword of the Spirit is used to pull down strongholds, a paddle is used to push and pull yourself through strong waters.

God's Word must be used with the proper practice and techniques. A paddle can make you faster and get you farther on the water, but only if you have practiced the proper technique for your paddle stroke.

Even though I was out on the river by myself this time in rougher waters and stronger currents, I knew I was not alone nor unequipped. God is always with me, and always provides me everything I need.

DAY 4:
Waiting on God's Perfect Timing

I wait for the Lord, my whole being waits,
and in his word I put my hope.
(Psalm 130:5 NIV)

One day, I was paddling on my own while one of my friends was taking the beginner SUP class. As I was heading into the river I noticed a man fishing from the bank. The problem was, he had lost one of his fishing poles, and was using his remaining pole to try to fish the lost one out of the water. He wasn't having any luck as it kept getting farther away from him.

I tried to get it for him with my paddle, but the fact that I was heading downstream and would have to get into an area of shallow water to retrieve it, made it an impossible task without risking falling off the board near some rocks. I apologized for not being able to help and continued on my way.

Later, as I turned around to head upstream back to the marina, I spotted the fishing pole. It had floated to a deeper area of the river where I was now able to maneuver my board easily and safely pull it out of the water. I tucked the pole under the cargo bungees and headed back to where I first found the fisherman, hoping he was still there. He was, and he was happy to see his fishing pole again. Because of its length, I was able to hand it over to him without getting too close to the shallow edges of the bank.

There are a lot of things in this life I want to find. Things I've lost, things I'm still looking for. But something I'm at peace with is the knowledge that those things will happen in God's perfect timing: when they don't have to be forced, at the right time, and in the right place.

The second time I saw the fishing pole, it was so much easier for me to get it because this time it was floating toward me instead of away from me. I didn't have to try to go after it.

Another connection I noted was that, yes, paddling upstream exerts a little more energy, but when you're looking up toward God, you can see that every good and perfect gift is from above, coming down from the Father (James 1:17). When you're looking down or heading in the wrong direction, or even spending time in shallow waters, you're likely to stumble and fall.

> *One day as Jesus was standing by the Lake of Gennesaret, the people were crowding around him and listening to the word of God. He saw at the water's edge two boats, left there by the fishermen, who were washing their nets. He got into one of the boats, the one be-*

longing to Simon, and asked him to put out a little from shore. Then he sat down and taught the people from the boat.

When he had finished speaking, he said to Simon, "Put out into deep water, and let down the nets for a catch."

Simon answered, "Master, we've worked hard all night and haven't caught anything. But because you say so, I will let down the nets."

When they had done so, they caught such a large number of fish that their nets began to break. So they signaled their partners in the other boat to come and help them, and they came and filled both boats so full that they began to sink.

When Simon Peter saw this, he fell at Jesus' knees and said, "Go away from me, Lord; I am a sinful man!" For he and all his companions were astonished at the catch of fish they had taken, and so were James and John, the sons of Zebedee, Simon's partners.

Then Jesus said to Simon, "Don't be afraid; from now on you will fish for people." So they pulled their boats up on shore, left everything and followed him. (Luke 5:1-11 NIV)

These fishermen had been working hard in their own time with no results, but when Jesus told them the time was right, their reward was vast. When we follow Him and trust in His timing, we can receive blessings not only for ourselves, but for those we help along the way.

SUP: SPIRITUAL UNDERSTANDING & PRAYER

DAY 5:
Remain Standing Tall

*We've been surrounded and battered
by troubles, but we're not demoralized;
we're not sure what to do, but we know
that God knows what to do...God
hasn't left our side.*
(2 Corinthians 4:8-9 MSG)

One evening I went out for a mid-week paddle. I was part of a group of about seven stand up paddlers and got to try out some new turns on the board. While out on the river, three boisterous guys in a fishing boat came speeding past us. Our group overheard them saying, "Hey let's knock them off their boards."

They circled around us a few times trying to create enough wake to make us fall, but no such luck for them. We all stayed standing. Little did the boaters know the boards we were on are made specifically for the surf, so handling their small waves was a piece of cake. Plus, we all have pretty good balance.

But, dear friends, remember what the apostles of our Lord Jesus Christ foretold. They said to you, "In the last times there will be scoffers who will follow their own ungodly desires." These are the people who divide you, who follow mere natural instincts and do not have the Spirit. But you, dear friends, by building yourselves up in your most holy faith and praying in the Holy Spirit, keep yourselves in God's love as you wait for the mercy of our Lord Jesus Christ to bring you to eternal life. Be merciful to those who doubt; save others by snatching them from the fire; to others show mercy, mixed with fear—hating even the clothing stained by corrupted flesh. To him who is able to keep you from stumbling and to present you be-fore his glorious presence without fault and with great joy—to the only God our Savior be glory, majesty, power and authority, through Jesus Christ our Lord, before all ages, now and forevermore! Amen.

(Jude 17-25 NIV)

There will always be people who will try to knock you off your game or make you stumble and fall. But, as long as you are properly equipped to handle it, and you keep a balanced outlook on life with Christ at the center, you can remain standing tall.

DAY 6:
Light and Narrow

*Small is the gate and narrow the road
that leads to life, and only a few find it.
(Matthew 7:14 NIV)*

I finally decided to stop renting a SUP board and instead buy my own. After doing a lot of online research, I took the time to "test drive" a few boards at the local SUP shop. The co-owner of the shop was so helpful and really took his time to answer all my questions and let me try out several boards.

One board in particular was really narrow and therefore was not as easy to stand on as the others, but the weight of it was lighter than any other board. After being on it for a little while, the SUP pro told me, "Not many people can ride that board. It's not for everyone."

That statement, and the fact that it is the narrowest of the boards, made me think of the scripture about the Narrow Gate:

> *Enter through the narrow gate. For wide is the gate and broad is the road that leads to destruction, and many enter through it. But small is the gate and narrow the road that leads to life, and only a few find it.*
> *(Matthew 7:13-14 NIV)*

I discovered this narrow board was actually made for a child around twelve to thirteen years old, but the SUP owner often recommends it for someone with a small stature like mine. That explains why it's not for everyone. But I've put away childish things (1 Corinthians 13:11) and therefore did not purchase that board.

Instead, I purchased a 12'6" race board that was still narrow compared to a recreational board, but was perfect for my size and more stable. However, before I signed on the dotted line, I wanted to take it into the harbor alone and pray over the decision. I sat on the board, asking the Lord if I should use my money for such a big purchase. I wanted to be sure I wasn't making a decision with my flesh.

His answer was to purchase the board and use it to bring glory to His name. Jesus has helped me do just that by providing the inspiration for my blog, this book, and my work with my clients.

DAY 7:
God is My Help

*Surely God is my help; the Lord is
the one who sustains me.
(Psalm 54:4 NIV)*

From where I store and launch my SUP board, there is a sensor at the end of the building that rings a bell inside the SUP shop when someone floats by it on his or her board. This alerts the workers inside that someone is coming in from a paddle and may need help getting the board out of the water and into its designated storage spot.

When I first got my own board, I was able to get it out of the water by myself, but trying to get it back in its storage spot was a little tough at first. Mainly because the board is long (12'6"), making it awkward to maneuver by hand without hitting and easily damaging the other boards stored so close together. For a few weeks, I needed help getting my board in and out of storage.

Sometimes in my life, there are things going on that are just too much for me to handle on my own. If I try to handle it all by myself, I end up "dropping the ball" on things or "just hitting a wall." I'm so fortunate that my Heavenly Father knows when I need help and alerts the right people to step in and be of assistance.

Just like I can't hear when the bell goes off inside the SUP shop as I'm paddling in, I can't hear or know when God is getting ready to send help. I just have to trust that He hears my cry for help or knows my need for help even before I do.

A certain woman of the wives of the sons of the prophets cried out to Elisha, saying, "Your servant my husband is dead, and you know that your servant feared the Lord. And the creditor is coming to take my two sons to be his slaves."

So Elisha said to her, "What shall I do for you? Tell me, what do you have in the house?" And she said, "Your maidservant has nothing in the house but a jar of oil."

Then he said, "Go, borrow vessels from everywhere, from all your neighbors— empty vessels; do not gather just a few. And when you have come in, you shall shut the door behind you and your sons; then pour it into all those vessels, and set aside the full ones."

So she went from him and shut the door behind her and her sons, who brought the vessels to her; and she poured it out.

SUP: SPIRITUAL UNDERSTANDING & PRAYER

Now it came to pass, when the vessels were full, that she said to her son, "Bring me another vessel."

And he said to her, "There is not another vessel." So the oil ceased. Then she came and told the man of God. And he said, "Go, sell the oil and pay your debt; and you and your sons live on the rest." (2 Kings 4: 1-7 NIV)

Asking for help isn't always easy. But I'm never ashamed or hesitant to ask God. I just have to remember to be open to and accepting of the help He sends me through other people. And, when it is necessary to go to others, I need to find that humility and also use wisdom in seeking out people I can trust. In every case—whether God directly helps me, sends a helper to me, or shows me I am to ask another for help—the Lord is always my comfort and support.

DAY 8:
Go With the Flow

Anyone who believes in me may come and drink! For the Scriptures declare, "Rivers of living water will flow from his heart."
(John 7:38 NLT)

Some days, the current on the river is stronger than other days. When that's the case, I head upstream so I won't have to exert as much effort in the latter half of my paddle when I'm already some-what fatigued.

When going against a strong current, I can feel myself quickly moving backward when I stop for a sip of water or to take in the scenery. After I reach a certain point, sometimes I rest for a bit by sit-ting on my board and letting the current do all the work to carry me back down-stream.

There are times in life when it's best to stop fighting against God and give it all over to Him, letting Him lead our lives out of the overflowing goodness of His heart.

God is our refuge and strength,
    an ever-present help in trouble.
Therefore we will not fear, though the
earth give way
        and the mountains fall into the heart
        of the sea,
though its waters roar and foam
        and the mountains quake with their
        surging.
There is a river whose streams make glad
the city of God,
        the holy place where the Most High
        dwells.
God is within her, she will not fall;
        God will help her at break of day.
He says, "Be still, and know that I am
God;
        I will be exalted among the nations,
        I will be exalted in the earth."

The Lord Almighty is with us;

the God of Jacob is our fortress.

(Psalm 46:1-5, 10-11 NIV)

God is strong, powerful, and in control.
We can let ourselves be guided by Him.
We don't always have to be in control.
We can be still and let Him lead.

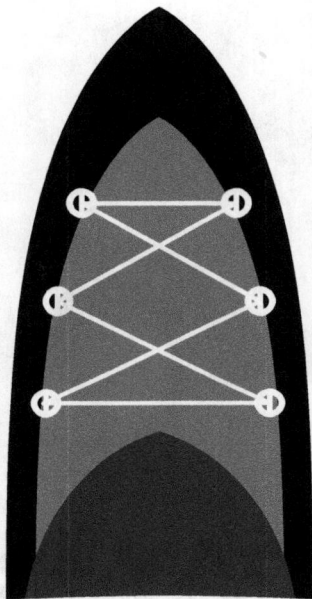

GROWTH

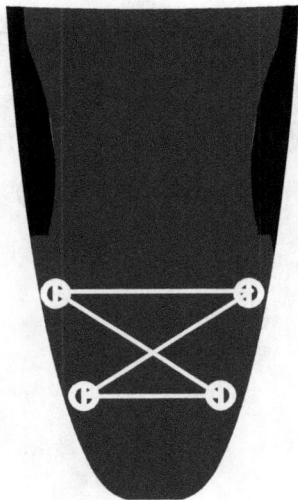

GROWTH

DAY 9:
What Are Your Gifts?

God has given each of you a gift from his great variety of spiritual gifts. Use them well to serve one another.
(1 Peter 4:10 NLT)

After about two months of learning how to SUP (and a few weeks after purchasing my own board), I was called into a meeting with the co-owner of the SUP shop. He didn't say what the meeting was about, so my curiosity was piqued. When I went in to see him, he asked if I'd be interested in helping out on the weekends with teaching first-time paddlers.

I was very honored at his request since I'd only been paddling for a short while. I was also very excited because teaching and encouraging others are two of my top spiritual gifts. If you've never taken a spiritual gifts assessment, I recommend you do so (www.spiritualgiftstest.com). It's a cool thing to do because it helps you better understand how God has uniquely equipped you to serve Him and His children.

After enthusiastically agreeing to the co-owner's request, I immediately received an intensive crash-course on being a SUP instructor. I began under the owner's watchful eye, and while the teaching part came easy, handling all the different boards (loading them onto the docks, launching them, etc.) was a little awkward at first.

Spiritual gifts can be utilized in a number of ways and settings, not just inside a church building or in a traditional mission field. I see opportunities around me every day in my own career coaching business to utilize my gifting. If you're employed in a job that matches your spiritual gifts, then you're in a good place. If your job requirements don't match up with your gifts, perhaps there are volunteer opportunities that do where you can fulfill your natural talents.

Therefore, I urge you, brothers and sisters, in view of God's mercy, to offer your bodies as a living sacrifice, holy and pleasing to God—this is your true and proper worship. Do not conform to the pattern of this world, but be transformed by the renewing of your mind. Then you will be able to test and approve what God's will is—his good, pleasing and perfect will. For by the grace given me I say to every one of you: Do not think of yourself more highly than you ought, but rather think of yourself with sober judgment, in accordance with the faith God has distributed to each of you. For just as each of us has one body with many members, and these members do not all have the same function, so in Christ we, though many, form one body, and each member belongs to all the others. We have different gifts, according to the grace

given to each of us. If your gift is proph-
esying, then prophesy in accordance
with your faith; if it is serving, then serve;
if it is teaching, then teach; if it is to
encourage, then give encouragement;
if it is giving, then give generously; if it
is to lead, do it diligently; if it is to show
mercy, do it cheerfully.
(Romans 12:1-8 NIV)

What are your spiritual gifts? How are
you using them to further God's kingdom?

DAY 10:
Get Down on Your Knees

Get down on your knees before the Master; it's the only way you'll get on your feet.
(James 4:10 MSG)

During my training to become an instructor for the beginner SUP class, I had to learn what to do if something goes wrong while giving lessons. While the likelihood of having a situation where someone falls off his or her board and starts drowning or goes unconscious is very minimal, I'm required to know how to get the paddler back on his or her board.

I was rather nervous at the thought of practicing this for the first time, especially since the man I was "rescuing" was a foot taller than I am and more than twice my weight. It seemed a bit impossible to me to be able to pull his dead weight up onto a board while I was in the water, until I was shown how it was done and tried it. I succeeded in the first try. For nothing is impossible with God (Luke 1:37).

SUP: SPIRITUAL UNDERSTANDING & PRAYER

Thank goodness I learned how to do this because the very next day could have easily been one of those occasions where something went wrong. I was one of three people taking a group of nine beginner paddlers out to the river. I was bringing up the rear, and just as we were about to exit the harbor and enter into the river, one of the young girls at the back of the group said she suddenly felt faint and was seeing spots.

I told her if she wanted to return to the docks to get some water and relax until the feeling passed, I would go back with her, but the immediate need was for her to get down on her knees on the board. If she remained standing and fainted, she would have likely fallen and hit her head on the board. Getting back on her knees lowered her center of gravity, made her feel less faint, and kept her safe from falling. We made it back to the docks without incident, thank God.

> *So let God work his will in you. Yell a*
> *loud no to the Devil and watch him*
> *scamper. Say a quiet yes to God and*
> *he'll be there in no time. Quit dabbling*
> *in sin. Purify your inner life. Quit playing*
> *the field. Hit bottom, and cry your eyes*
> *out. The fun and games are over. Get*
> *serious, really serious. Get down on your*
> *knees before the Master; it's the only*
> *way you'll get on your feet.*
> *(James 4:7-10 MSG)*

When life makes us feel unstable, the best thing we can do is hit our knees and cry out to God. He will stabilize our emotions and give us peace.

DAY 11:
Digging Deep

*Son of man, let all my words sink
deep into your own heart first. Listen
to them carefully for yourself.
(Ezekiel 3:10 NLT)*

Once I began teaching the beginner SUP class, I noticed that I often had to remind new paddlers to always dig the face of the paddle deep into the water so that it's completely submersed. Not putting it fully in the water is one of the biggest mistakes beginner paddlers make, causing them to move slower through the water.

One of the biggest mistakes many new (and not so new) believers make is not taking time to dig deep into the Word on a daily basis. Relying on a scriptural sermon for less than an hour a week on Sundays only skims the surface of what God wants to say to each of us personally, and can cause us to move slower in our spiritual walk.

Up until about eight years ago, I didn't spend time in the Word on a daily basis.

SUP: SPIRITUAL UNDERSTANDING & PRAYER

Now, I can't imagine a day without it. It's as important to my day as eating breakfast or even breathing.

God has revealed so much to me in these past eight years because I have taken the time to listen to Him, and I want to continue listening to Him.

Why do you call me, "Lord, Lord," and do not do what I say? As for everyone who comes to me and hears my words and puts them into practice, I will show you what they are like. They are like a man building a house, who dug down deep and laid the foundation on rock. When a flood came, the torrent struck that house but could not shake it, because it was well built. But the one who hears my words and does not put them into practice is like a man who built a house on the ground without a founda-

tion. The moment the torrent struck that house, it collapsed and its destruction was complete.
(Luke 6:46-49 NIV)

Have you made time in your day to dig deep and hear what He wants to say to you? Shallowness will slow your journey to truth. Depth will give you an unshakeable faith.

DAY 12:
Taming the Tongue

And a tiny rudder makes a huge ship turn wherever the pilot wants it to go, even though the winds are strong. So also, the tongue is a small thing, but what enormous damage it can do.
(James 3:4-5 NLT)

Oftentimes if I'm paddling on the Cumberland River, a huge barge will come by. It's important to stay out of a barge's way since they are much like trains in that they cannot stop on a dime.

But what's even more interesting is that barges don't create a lot of noise in the water. You would think something that big would create a loud wake, but it doesn't. However, that doesn't mean they're not churning up a lot of stuff far below the water's surface.

Even if words are spoken quietly or in a non-threatening tone, they can still have a profound effect on someone and churn up things for the receiver of those words in ways the speaker cannot see or imagine. And once something is spoken, it cannot be taken back—its effects cannot be stopped.

SUP: SPIRITUAL UNDERSTANDING & PRAYER

My tongue is one of the hardest things for me to control. There are so many things I have said in my life that I wish I could take back. I'm thankful for God's grace and forgiveness for the words I have spoken, and I pray for His grace to help me better control something that's often so untamable in my own strength.

Remember that we are not fighting the tongue's fire in our own strength. The Holy Spirit will give us increasing power to monitor and control what we say, so that when we are offended, the Spirit will remind us of God's love, and we won't react in a hateful manner. When we are criticized, the Spirit will heal the hurt, and we won't lash out.
(James 3:8 study note from the Life Application Bible)

DAY 13:
Do Not Worry

Look at the birds of the air; they do not sow or reap or store away in barns, and yet your heavenly Father feeds them. Are you not much more valuable than they? Can any one of you by worrying add a single hour to your life?
(Matthew 6:26-27 NIV)

My favorite way to destress is to take a leisurely paddle and just soak in all the sights and sounds of the surrounding nature: listening to the birds chirp and the fish splash as they brave the surface of the water, watching the turtles sunning themselves on branches sticking out of the river, and watching a blue heron fly across the horizon in front of me. The blue herons are so beautiful.

One day I spotted a giant bird's nest in a tree top. It was the largest nest I've ever seen. I'm not sure if it was the nest of a heron, but it was definitely of something similar in size. I was thinking how easy the animals have it. They don't have the same kind of complicated concerns we as humans have. But then I was reminded how we really don't have as much to worry about as we think we do.

SUP: SPIRITUAL UNDERSTANDING & PRAYER

Therefore I tell you, do not worry about your life, what you will eat or drink; or about your body, what you will wear. Is not life more than food, and the body more than clothes? Look at the birds of the air; they do not sow or reap or store away in barns, and yet your heavenly Father feeds them. Are you not much more valuable than they? Can any one of you by worrying add a single hour to your life? And why do you worry about clothes? See how the flowers of the field grow. They do not labor or spin. Yet I tell you that not even Solomon in all his splendor was dressed like one of these. If that is how God clothes the grass of the field, which is here today and tomorrow is thrown into the fire, will he not much more clothe you—you of little faith? So do not worry, saying, "What shall we eat?" or "What shall we drink?" or "What shall we wear?" For the pa-

gans run after all these things, and your heavenly Father knows that you need them. But seek first his kingdom and his righteousness, and all these things will be given to you as well. Therefore do not worry about tomorrow, for tomor-row will worry about itself. Each day has enough trouble of its own.
(Matthew 6:25-34 NIV)

What are the things you unnecessarily worry about in your life?

DAY 14:
Unharmed

*You'll walk unharmed among lions
and snakes, and kick young lions and
serpents from the path.
(Psalm 91:13 MSG)*

One day following a paddle down the river, I decided to take my board into the harbor and just sit and reflect on some things. As I was sitting there, I happened to see something ahead in the water. Immediately I knew what it was before I even got a closer look...something I had not yet seen while paddleboarding, something I never desired to see because of my phobia. It was a snake.

Just to be certain, I stood back up on my board and paddled a little closer for a better look. Yep, it was a water moccasin. I don't know much about water moccasins other than they are poisonous. When I told a couple of people what I saw, they warned me that water moccasins are aggressive and will come after you. (One woman said she even saw one make a 180 and start coming straight for her boat!)

SUP: SPIRITUAL UNDERSTANDING & PRAYER

When I approached it, I noticed it was continuing to swim away from me instead of turning on me (thank God!). I was strangely calm despite my extreme fear of snakes. Perhaps that is because I know this truth:

You who sit down in the High God's presence, spend the night in Shaddai's shadow, Say this: "God, you're my refuge. I trust in you and I'm safe!" That's right—he rescues you from hidden traps, shields you from deadly hazards. His huge outstretched arms protect you—under them you're perfectly safe; his arms fend off all harm. Fear nothing—not wild wolves in the night, not flying arrows in the day, not disease that prowls through the darkness, not disaster that erupts at high noon. Even though others succumb all around, drop like flies right and left, no harm will

even graze you. You'll stand untouched, watch it all from a distance, watch the wicked turn into corpses. Yes, because God's your refuge, the High God your very own home, evil can't get close to you, harm can't get through the door. He ordered his angels to guard you wherever you go. If you stumble, they'll catch you; their job is to keep you from falling. You'll walk unharmed among lions and snakes, and kick young lions and serpents from the path.
(Psalm 91:1-13 MSG)

What are you afraid of? Are you trusting God's protection from your fear?

DAY 15:
Against the Wind

If any of you lacks wisdom, you should ask God, who gives generously to all without finding fault, and it will be given to you. But when you ask, you must believe and not doubt, because the one who doubts is like a wave of the sea, blown and tossed by the wind.
(James 1:5-6 NIV)

I went out for a paddle on a day that was very windy. So windy it almost felt like the beach, and the gusts were kicking up some pretty good waves in the river.

I decided to head downstream because I had a strong headwind going in that direction, much stronger than the downstream current. Knowing it would require extra strength to paddle in that headwind, I also understood I'd have a strong tailwind to bring me back upstream.

The tailwind was so strong on my return that I didn't even really have to paddle. The breeze just guided me safely back upstream to the harbor. If I hadn't been accurately able to discern the direction of the wind, I could have gone the opposite direction and been more fatigued coming back against a headwind after having already had a long paddle.

SUP: SPIRITUAL UNDERSTANDING & PRAYER

Sometimes in life, we have headwinds we have to face, ones that make us work harder but also can make us stronger. Other times, getting through life is a breeze. This is the reality of living in this world. It's good, though, to gain wisdom and discernment on what direction the wind is coming from.

Sometimes when we're struggling against a headwind, it's because we're trying to do something God doesn't intend for us to do (and that "something" is also probably leading us the opposite direction from Him). Other times, the direction of the struggle can be coming from Satan because he wants to discourage us and cause us to give up on the good thing we're working so hard for. Consequently, just because some things are a breeze doesn't necessarily mean they are within God's will. Doing God's will is not always easy or comfortable.

> If a prophet, or one who foretells by dreams, appears among you and announces to you a sign or wonder, and if the sign or wonder spoken of takes place, and the prophet says, "Let us follow other gods" (gods you have not known) "and let us worship them," you must not listen to the words of that prophet or dreamer. The Lord your God is testing you to find out whether you love him with all your heart and with all your soul. It is the Lord your God you must follow, and him you must revere. Keep his commands and obey him; serve him and hold fast to him. (Deuteronomy 13:1-4 NIV)

In everything we are to seek God's wisdom and to pray for discernment so that we can determine if a headwind or a tailwind is from Him or from the enemy. Anything that's from the enemy is the WRONG direction. Anything that's from Jesus our Savior is the RIGHT direction.

Are you asking God for wisdom and discernment on which direction you should go?

DAY 16:
Lifting Up
Our Fellow Man

*For if they fall, one will lift up his fellow.
But woe to him who is alone when he
falls and has not another to lift him up!
(Ecclesiastes 4:10 ESV)*

In late September, the water is so favorable. Although slightly chilly, it's typically very smooth and calm. This truly is one of the best times of year to paddle. One late September evening I was out on a paddle by myself, and then, as I was heading back to the harbor, I saw a group that included one of the guys I worked with at the SUP shop. He and his best friend had both of their mothers visiting and were taking them out for a paddle. They invited me to join them so I stayed out a little longer.

Since the mothers were new at the sport, they were still trying to learn how to balance, and both of them ended up falling in the river. Of course the sons were laughing at their moms, but the moms were laughing too because they were having such a great time and had a good sense of humor about it.

SUP: SPIRITUAL UNDERSTANDING & PRAYER

Then, one of the sons fell in. I laughed at him, and then immediately thought, I'm probably going in next since I'm amused at his mishap. And since I'd just passed a man standing on his dock who asked, "Isn't the water cold tonight?" and had replied with, "I don't know, I haven't been in it," I knew it was just a matter of time.

I'd gone probably four miles that evening without going in the water. In fact I've never fallen in the river, only in the harbor while practicing step turns on my board and goofing off, thoroughly expecting to end up in the water in those situations. That night, I was almost home free to the mouth of the harbor after my long paddle, and all of a sudden, in trying to maneuver my board past one of the sons, I went right in.

To answer the man on the dock's question, yes, the water was cold, but it was exhilarating. At this point we were all laughing at and with each other. But not only had we joked with each other throughout the paddle, we also encouraged each other, helped each other up, and made sure each of us was okay.

Therefore, brothers and sisters, since we have confidence to enter the Most Holy Place by the blood of Jesus, by a new and living way opened for us through the curtain, that is, his body, and since we have a great priest over the house of God, let us draw near to God with a sincere heart and with the full assurance that faith brings, having our hearts sprinkled to cleanse us from a guilty conscience and having our bodies washed with pure water. Let us hold unswervingly to the hope we profess, for

he who promised is faithful. And let us consider how we may spur one another on toward love and good deeds, not giving up meeting together, as some are in the habit of doing, but encouraging one another—and all the more as you see the Day approaching.
(Hebrews 10:19-25 NIV)

We all fall sometimes, but God brings people into our lives to help lift us up, whether it's through laughter, encouragement, or physical strength.

DAY 17:
New Friends

After Job had prayed for his friends, the
LORD restored his fortunes and gave him
twice as much as he had before.
(Job 42:10 NIV)

God always knows when I need a friend. Oftentimes He has shown me there are people here for me even when it doesn't feel like it. He always knows when to introduce me to someone new who seems like someone I've known much longer.

One day while paddling, I got to know another board owner who loves SUP as much as I do. We went out for a paddle together when the water was rather calm. That calm water allowed us to talk to each other without distraction and get to know each other better.

Come to find out, we've both experienced some of the same struggles, including the loss of our mothers to cancer, major career transitions, life before accepting God, and more. Even though we didn't really know each other that well, we both felt like we could open up to each other and share things that we wouldn't ordinarily share with a stranger.

Again I saw something meaningless under the sun:
There was a man all alone;
*   he had neither son nor brother.*
There was no end to his toil,
*   yet his eyes were not content with his wealth.*
"For whom am I toiling," he asked,
*   "and why am I depriving myself of enjoyment?"*
This too is meaningless—
*   a miserable business!*
Two are better than one,
*   because they have a good return for their labor:*
If either of them falls down,
*   one can help the other up.*
But pity anyone who falls
*   and has no one to help them up.*

Also, if two lie down together, they will keep warm.

But how can one keep warm alone?
Though one may be overpowered,
two can defend themselves.
A cord of three strands is not quickly broken.
(Ecclesiastes 4:7-12 NIV)

Maybe we felt we could open up because of the calming effect water has on our spirits, or because we are sisters in Christ, or both. Either way, God knows when we need a friend, and He is here to provide.

"Friendship multiplies the good of life and divides the evil." Baltasar Gracian

DAY 18:
Persevering When Tempted to Give Up

Therefore, since we are surrounded by such a great cloud of witnesses, let us throw off everything that hinders and the sin that so easily entangles. And let us run with perseverance the race marked out for us, fixing our eyes on Jesus, the pioneer and perfecter of faith.
(Hebrews 12:1-2 NIV)

The owners of the SUP shop invited a group of us to go out for a mileage builder on a day when the current was quite swift (about 3 MPH). The plan was to paddle downstream to the next harbor, and then back upstream against the fast current for a total of 8 miles round trip. The owner said, "It will be great training!" So I said, "Let's do it!"

There were some eddies in the water and some swells from a barge ahead of us, but otherwise it was an uncomplicated paddle downstream. We were moving rather rapidly, and it only took us half an hour to get to the other harbor. Despite the ease of the first leg, we all knew going back was going to be much, much tougher.

What took us half an hour going downstream turned into two and a half hours going upstream. We felt like we were on a treadmill or trying to advance the opposite way on an escalator. When we finally came in view of our final destination, it seemed like a mirage because it felt like we'd never reach it.

My hands began blistering, and all of us were experiencing fatigue. But giving up was not an option. We had to keep paddling and keep our eye on our destination. If we stopped for even just a moment, we would lose a lot of the ground we had gained. Once we finally made it back, we felt stronger, like we could accomplish anything!

Therefore, since we have been justified through faith, we have peace with God through our Lord Jesus Christ, through whom we have gained access by faith into this grace in which we now stand.

And we boast in the hope of the glory of God. Not only so, but we also glory in our sufferings, because we know that suffering produces perseverance; perseverance, character; and character, hope. And hope does not put us to shame, because God's love has been poured out into our hearts through the Holy Spirit, who has been given to us.
(Romans 5:1-5 NIV)

Never give up on your God-given goals. Instead, seek God's strength to help you persevere.

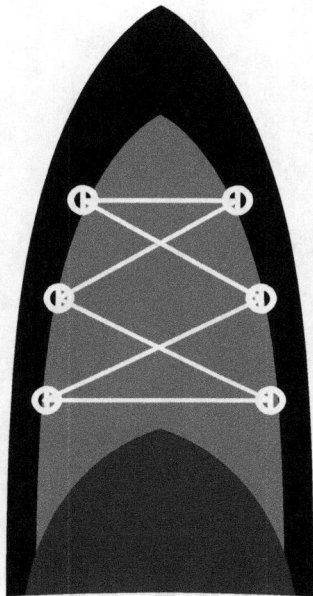

MOMENTUM

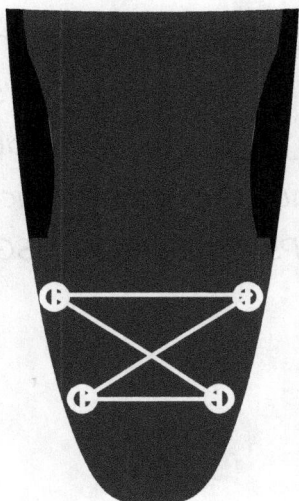

DAY 19:
And Suddenly
It Happened

Suddenly, God, you floodlight my life;
I'm blazing with glory, God's glory! I
smash the bands of marauders, I
vault the highest fences.
(Psalm 18:28-29 MSG)

One day I had a personal best on my board. It was the fastest I had ever gone up to that point. To my surprise, I was able not only to keep up with one of the co-owners of the SUP shop, but even stay somewhat ahead of her. I told her she must be having an off day...either that or the thirty pound dog on her board was slowing her down. She said, "Lori, give yourself more credit than that! You're upping your game and improving greatly!" Her encouragement felt good to hear.

When I first took up SUP, I wasn't trying to compete with myself or with anyone else. My goal was to better myself so I could better enjoy the sport. But to discover that I'd advanced that much without even really trying just goes to show that if you are consistent with something, you will improve. And like most other sports or activities, you usually do better when you participate with others who are better than you. I've found this to be true in the past with other activities I've enjoyed such as dance and rock climbing.

On this particular day, it felt like something just clicked and I hit my stride in such a natural way. It wasn't anything I was trying to do in my own power. It just suddenly happened.

> *You then, my son, be strong in the grace that is in Christ Jesus. And the things you have heard me say in the presence of many witnesses entrust to reliable people who will also be qualified to teach others. Join with me in suffering, like a good soldier of Christ Jesus...anyone who competes as an athlete does not receive the victor's crown except by competing according to the rules. The*

*hardworking farmer should be the first
to receive a share of the crops...There-
fore I endure everything for the sake of
the elect, that they too may obtain the
salvation that is in Christ Jesus, with
eternal glory.*
(2 Timothy 2:1-3, 5-6, 10 NIV)

*Love must be sincere. Hate what is evil;
cling to what is good. Be devoted to
one another in love. Honor one another above yourselves. Never be lacking
in zeal, but keep your spiritual fervor,
serving the Lord. Be joyful in hope, patient in affliction, faithful in prayer. Share
with the Lord's people who are in need.
Practice hospitality. Bless those who
persecute you; bless and do not curse.
Rejoice with those who rejoice; mourn
with those who mourn. Live in harmony
with one another.*
(Romans 12:9-16 NIV)

SUP: SPIRITUAL UNDERSTANDING & PRAYER

This serves as a reminder that we need to remain persistent in our spiritual walk and surround ourselves with people who challenge us, hold us accountable, and help us grow stronger in our walk with Christ. When we do, God can suddenly give us His power to accomplish things we never thought possible.

DAY 20:
Seagulls on the Cumberland

*Are not two sparrows sold for a penny?
Yet not one of them will fall to the ground
outside your Father's care. And even the
very hairs of your head are all numbered.
So don't be afraid; you are worth
more than many sparrows.
(Matthew 10:29-31 NIV)*

When paddling in the winter, I often notice the presence of seagulls on the Cumberland River. After doing a little research on the symbolic meaning of seagulls, here's what I found:

- Seagulls often show up at places other than the beach because they go where they can find the best food. This serves as a reminder for us to move out of our comfort zones in order to gain access to better resources. We shouldn't deny ourselves opportunities just because we feel safe in our comfort zones.
   - *All hard work brings a profit, but mere talk leads only to poverty. The wealth of the wise is their crown, but the folly of fools yields folly.*
   (Proverbs 14:23-24 NIV)

SUP: SPIRITUAL UNDERSTANDING & PRAYER

- The word "gull" is the root word of "gullible." While seagulls will migrate outside of their comfort zone to find the best food, they also will gulp down anything available to them without much consideration. This is a reminder that, unlike the seagull, we should not jump at every opportunity or believe everything that's being fed to us through our eyes and our ears. Instead we should use the wisdom and discernment God has given us when picking through information and options.

    - *What sorrow awaits those who look to Egypt for help, trusting their horses, chariots, and charioteers and depending on the strength of human armies instead of looking to the Lord, the Holy One of Israel.*
    (Isaiah 31:1-3 NLT)

- Seagulls are not afraid to squawk and make a lot of noise. We too should be fearless about finding our voices and speaking our minds.
  - *For the Spirit God gave us does not make us timid, but gives us power, love and self-discipline. So do not be ashamed of the testimony about our Lord or of me his prisoner. Rather, join with me in suffering for the gospel, by the power of God.*
    (2 Timothy 1:7-8 NIV)

- In some cultures the seagull is a symbol of freedom, which reminds us that there is freedom in relationship with God. When we surrender our lives to Him, we become free of sin, guilt, and shame.
  - *[Give] joyful thanks to the Father, who has qualified you to share in*

the inheritance of his holy people in the kingdom of light. For he has rescued us from the dominion of darkness and brought us into the kingdom of the Son he loves, in whom we have redemption, the forgiveness of sins. (Colossians 1:12-14 NIV)

So, when you think of the seagull, think of nature and how God uses His creation to serve as examples for us. He provides food in various places for the seagull, and doesn't He care even more for us than He does the birds of this world?

DAY 21:
The Dangers of Ignoring Instruction

Trust in the Lord with all your heart and lean not on your own understanding; in all your ways submit to him, and he will make your paths straight.
(Proverbs 3:5, 6 NIV)

When the paddle season is in full swing, I see a lot more people trying SUP for the first time, which is great! But, there always seems to be a few newbies who, despite being instructed to stay out of the middle of the river, go right to the middle of the river and then lie on their boards and stay there. This can be dangerous, especially on days when there is a lot of boat or barge traffic.

This reminds me of the times in my life when I was told by my parents not to do certain things (i.e. like playing in the street). They gave me these instructions to protect me from various dangers. Our Heavenly Father also instructs His children in His Holy Word not to do certain things in order to protect us from the dangers of this world.

Now then, my children, listen to me;
blessed are those who keep my ways.
Listen to my instruction and be wise;
do not disregard it.
Blessed are those who listen to me,
watching daily at my doors,
waiting at my doorway.
For those who find me find life
and receive favor from the Lord.
But those who fail to find me harm
themselves;
all who hate me love death.
(Proverbs 8:32-36 NIV)

Someone recently shared with me a movie quote that says the Bible is not what it has been previously referred to by many, "Basic Instruction Before Leaving Earth," but instead it's God's love letter to us. Well, I say it's both, because a loving father shows his love in many ways, including providing his children with instruction to protect them from the dangers lurking in our world. (We know from Job 1:7 that Satan roams throughout the earth.)

There can be both subtle and obvious consequences when choosing to ignore God's instruction. These consequences aren't necessarily God punishing us, but instead they can be the natural occurrence after we choose to open ourselves up to the evil from which He is trying to protect us. (First Peter 5:8 says Satan is poised to pounce.)

There are plenty examples of this in the Bible, especially among the Israelites when they chose to ignore God's command not to put other gods before Him and instead adopted some of the pagan practices of the surrounding nations. You could probably say they were "playing in the middle of the street" (or the middle of the river!) by dabbling in those forbidden practices. We should never forget what Proverbs 3:5-6 says: *Trust in the Lord with all your heart and lean not on your own understanding; in all your ways submit to him, and he will make your paths straight. (NIV)*

DAY 22:
Let Light Shine Out of Darkness

For God, who said, "Let light shine out of darkness," made his light shine in our hearts to give us the light of the knowledge of God's glory displayed in the face of Christ.
(2 Corinthians 4:6 NIV)

A group of paddlers always goes out to paddle during nights when there's a full moon. One particular night, it was a blue moon, and conditions were perfect.

As our group paddled out, the sun was still setting, and the direction we went gave us a beautiful view of the sunset. Once the light was almost gone, we turned around to see the huge moon rising up over the horizon in the opposite direction.

It gave me comfort to know that, even when times seem dark, God's light always shines through. Even if it's just a hint from a far-away star, or from the fullest of moons. God's light shone that night, in the setting sun, the rising moon, and even in the shooting star we witnessed after returning from our paddle.

SUP: SPIRITUAL UNDERSTANDING & PRAYER

Give thanks to the Lord of lords:
His love endures forever.
to him who alone does great wonders,
His love endures forever.
who by his understanding made the
heavens,
His love endures forever.
who spread out the earth upon the
waters,
His love endures forever.
who made the great lights—
His love endures forever.
the sun to govern the day,
His love endures forever.
the moon and stars to govern the night;
His love endures forever.
(Psalm 136:3-9 NIV)

DAY 23:
The Encouragement of Solitude

But Jesus Himself would often slip away
to the wilderness and pray.
(Luke 5:16 NASB)

One of my spiritual gifts is the gift of encouragement. In every type of professional work I've done, I've been able to use my gift to serve my clients and my students. Likewise, in certain friendships and relationships, I've had the opportunity to give comfort and confidence to others in times of sorrow and anxiety, and have also had it reciprocated. To get to operate in my spiritual gift is an encouragement to me.

I remember listening to a podcast series by a well-respected pastor on the topic of encouragement. He said that people are in more need of reassurance and relief today than ever in the history of the world. He described different ways we can be an encouragement to others, and how we can be an encouragement to ourselves when we need it most. He said one way we can reassure and restore ourselves is through solitude.

Solitude may be something some people are uncomfortable with, but I've learned to relish it, even when I don't feel like being alone. Here's what the pastor had to say about solitude:

> *God used certain people in a mighty way, but before He could, He had to teach them to be alone, teach them what isolation was all about. There is ministry in solitude and if we don't learn how to cultivate that, we will have a very difficult time encouraging ourselves in the Lord. To be quiet so you can talk to God and so God can talk to you. King David understood the importance of getting alone, and so did Jesus. If a man considers his time to be so valuable that he cannot find time to keep quiet and*

*to be alone, that man will eventually be
of no value to anyone. To spend all of
one's time with people is soon to have
nothing to give any of them of any value.*
~Dr. David Jeremiah

For me, there are a few things I do in solitude that serve as a big encouragement for me. First and foremost, it's reading the Word at the start of each day and recording in my journal what I think God is saying to me through His Word, as if He were talking directly to me. *(Jesus said, "If you hold to my teaching, you are really my disciples. Then you will know the truth, and the truth will set you free." John 8:31-32 NIV)* When I later go back and read what I've recorded, it's often what I needed to be reminded of at exactly that point in time, or it's to confirm that He did what He promised He would do.

The sounds of nature are also an encouragement to me. Being alone outside, especially paddling on the water, is soothing for me. God's Word reminds me of the hope I have in Him, while being on the water makes me forget my sorrows and anxieties, at least for those few hours. The rhythm of the paddle strokes, coupled with the sounds of the water and the birds, make everything just melt away for me.

I love paddling on my own when I'm feeling discouraged (which was how I was feeling the day I wrote this). But I also enjoy paddling with a friend or a group who can also serve as an encouragement. I hope whoever is reading this is finding encouragement from the words God has put on my heart to share.

What are your own spiritual gifts? How are you using them, and are you getting encouragement from using them in various areas of your life? Spend some time in solitude to reflect on how you can better fulfill your purpose.

DAY 24:
The Encouragement of Others

Therefore encourage one another and build one another up, just as you are doing.
(I Thessalonians 5:11 NASB)

Yesterday I discussed how we can find encouragement in solitude. But, of course, we can also find encouragement from others.

One day, a fellow paddler and I went into the harbor to teach ourselves how to walk on our boards so we could perfect our turns, a challenging task for just about every paddler when first trying it. This is something I'd wanted to learn, and it was my goal to learn it before the end of the summer. So, I tried it.

At first, picking my feet up off the board felt nearly impossible. My feet felt glued to my board. I thought for sure I was going to lose my balance completely. But I knew I had to lift my foot and trust that, if I took that first step, God would guide me the rest of the way.

SUP: SPIRITUAL UNDERSTANDING & PRAYER

My fellow paddler and I would occasionally look over to see how the other was doing. She encouraged me as she saw me trying to walk. (I'm sure I looked like a baby deer taking its first steps.) And while it felt good to have encouragement from her, it felt even better to encourage her! She was progressing so well, and I kept saying, "There you go! You've got it!" Just saying those words to another person lifted my own spirits so high.

One of the things we both realized as we were trying these new techniques is that we had to go back to the basics, the things we learned the first time we ever stood on a board: don't look down (Remember, it was only after Peter looked down that he began to sink in Matthew 14:30.), and stabilize yourself with the paddle in the water.

While I still have more practice to do to be able to walk more confidently and more gracefully on my board, I felt like those first steps, though small and awkward, were a huge start. I started to feel "unstuck," and I don't think I would have tried as hard to make myself take those steps if there wasn't someone there by my side encouraging me and challenging me. When I'm feeling stuck in life, it helps me become unstuck when I have friends who encourage me as I take one scary, wobbly step at a time.

> *For God did not appoint us to suffer wrath but to receive salvation through our Lord Jesus Christ. He died for us so that, whether we are awake or asleep, we may live together with him. Therefore encourage one another and build each other up, just as in fact you are doing. Now we ask you, brothers and sisters,*

to acknowledge those who work hard among you, who care for you in the Lord and who admonish you. Hold them in the highest regard in love because of their work. Live in peace with each other. And we urge you, brothers and sisters, warn those who are idle and disruptive, encourage the disheartened, help the weak, be patient with everyone. Make sure that nobody pays back wrong for wrong, but always strive to do what is good for each other and for everyone else. Rejoice always, pray continually, give thanks in all circumstances; for this is God's will for you in Christ Jesus. (1 Thessalonians 5:9-18 NIV)

DAY 25:
Take Refuge

I long to dwell in your tent forever and take refuge in the shelter of your wings.
(Psalm 61:4 NIV)

Sometimes I like to paddle inside one of the coves along the riverside. I often do this on really blustery days when I need a little break from the wind. The cove shields me from the strong gusts on the open river, offering a temporary escape.

Inside the cove everything becomes so quiet and peaceful. I have to slow down my pace since there are a lot of tree branches and roots in the water to maneuver around. The peace and beauty inside my favorite cove is awesome. I can actually see the fish and the turtles in the water.

On one particularly windy day, I went as far back into the cove as I could get before fallen trees blocked my path. Once I reached that point, I just lay down on my board and soaked in all the peace and beauty.

SUP: SPIRITUAL UNDERSTANDING & PRAYER

This still moment reminded me of the many scriptures in the Psalms that refer to God as a refuge: a place of protection and solitude. Here I could get the quiet I needed to relish in some of God's beauty and be protected from the harsh winds of reality.

When you need to take refuge, reflect on these Scriptures:

> *But let all who take refuge in you be glad; let them ever sing for joy. Spread your protection over them, that those who love your name may rejoice in you. (Psalm 5:11 NIV)*

> *The Lord is a refuge for the oppressed, a stronghold in times of trouble. (Psalm 9:9 NIV)*

*Show me the wonders of your great love,
you who save by your right hand those
who take refuge in you from their foes.*
(Psalm 17:7 NIV)

*The Lord is my rock, my fortress and my
deliverer; my God is my rock, in whom I
take refuge, my shield and the horn of
my salvation, my stronghold.*
(Psalm 18:2 NIV)

*How abundant are the good things that
you have stored up for those who fear
you, that you bestow in the sight of all,
on those who take refuge in you.*
(Psalm 31:19 NIV)

*Taste and see that the Lord is good;
blessed is the one who takes refuge in
him.*
(Psalm 34:8 NIV)

SUP: SPIRITUAL UNDERSTANDING & PRAYER

*The righteous will rejoice in the Lord
and take refuge in him; all the upright in
heart will glory in him!
(Psalm 64:10 NIV)*

*Be my rock of refuge, to which I can al-
ways go; give the command to save me,
for you are my rock and my fortress.
(Psalm 71:3 NIV)*

*But as for me, it is good to be near God.
I have made the Sovereign Lord my ref-
uge; I will tell of all your deeds.
(Psalm 73:28 NIV)*

*I will say of the Lord, "He is my refuge
and my fortress, my God, in whom I
trust."
(Psalm 91:2 NIV)*

DAY 26:
Going the Distance

*I can do all things through Christ
who strengthens me.
(Philippians 4:13 NKJV)*

After only a year of doing SUP recreationally, I did something I never thought I could do. I paddled 16.4 miles from downtown Nashville back to the harbor where the paddle board shop is located. Now, I've never done any kind of runners' marathon before, nor have I ever had even the slightest desire to do so, but my love for stand up paddleboarding outweighed my general lack of interest in a long distance effort.

Even though this event was not a race, it was a personal challenge since at that point I'd only ever paddled seven to eight miles at the most. In the days leading up to this long-distance paddle, I prepared physically with mileage builders, strengthening exercises, and muscle stretches. But I knew I also had to prepare spiritually and mentally. I had my small group praying for my safety

SUP: SPIRITUAL UNDERSTANDING & PRAYER

and for strength. And I personally prayed for God's strength and for good weather conditions.

Despite the fact that our group had a head wind and little to no current to help carry us downstream faster, we accomplished the goal in a lot shorter time than we expected. I figured it would take five to six hours, but I finished in four hours and fifteen minutes! The weather was perfect. Temperatures were comfortable, and there were sunny skies even though the forecast predicted mostly clouds. (I had prayed for sunshine!)

Not only was I surprised at how quickly I completed the 16.4 miles, I was also surprised that I didn't start feeling tired until about mile 11. When the fatigue tried to set in, I just kept repeating to myself, "With Christ anything is possible," and "I can do all things through Christ who strengthens me."

With two miles left to go, I got my second wind. My muscles were hurting immediately after I finished. I thought for sure I would be sore the next day and would sleep like a rock that night. But, I tossed and turned from the adrenaline rush I was still on, and the next day I had only a little soreness in my triceps and my abs. I felt great!

In reflecting on the experience, I was trying to think what I would write for this entry. Then one of my clients sent me a devotional that described just what I was feeling all that time out there on my board. Here's an excerpt:

We can work out, have great biceps and abs. We can exercise our brains

SUP: SPIRITUAL UNDERSTANDING & PRAYER

and have great info and knowledge. But supernatural strength comes from the Lord, above and beyond our own abilities.

You are stronger than you think with God's help and power behind you. It is good to know where our inner strength comes from and who gives us that gift.

So how strong are you? Very strong, in Christ. And that is good news!

Inspirational Messages
Sally I. Kennedy, 2014

What can you do through Christ's strength?

DAY 27:
100 Miles of Motivation

Not that I have already obtained all this, or have already arrived at my goal, but I press on to take hold of that for which Christ Jesus took hold of me. Brothers and sisters, I do not consider myself yet to have taken hold of it. But one thing I do: Forgetting what is behind and straining toward what is ahead, I press on toward the goal to win the prize for which God has called me heavenward in Christ Jesus.

(Philippians 2:12-14 NIV)

Not long after the paddle from downtown Nashville, I joined something called the "Fit For Fall 100-Mile Paddle Challenge." It was a simple challenge between a group of us regular paddlers to paddle a total of 100 miles between October 12th and December 11th. I was hesitant at first to accept the challenge because I wasn't sure with the weather turning colder and the days getting shorter that I'd be able to complete the 100 miles within the allotted time frame. But, since it was for fun, I joined in without expecting to really care about my results.

I've never considered myself a very competitive person. But, as I started logging more and more miles with thanks to the great weather we were having, I became motivated to reach the goal. Not only did I complete the hundred miles, I did so by

SUP: SPIRITUAL UNDERSTANDING & PRAYER

November 11th, one full month before the challenge ended. I came in 3rd place out of ten paddlers, coming in at a total of 106.7 miles. This was a good feeling, but even better than that was the experience of getting to know the other challenge participants at a deeper level while out there paddling together, working toward a common goal.

There were a lot of days when I was paddling by myself, but also several days where I was with one or more people. This gave me the opportunity to talk with and learn more about them. It was the one-on-one paddles that led to the deeper conversations which seemed to naturally gravitate toward topics of faith.

Our conversations weren't about the paddle challenge, but instead about the challenges we were each facing in life. It was encouraging to know I wasn't the only one facing similar difficulties. And it was an opportunity to be an encouragement to them too.

Even after the challenge ended, I've continued to invest in the new relationships this fun past-time has brought into my life. Who knew the "Fit For Fall" objective would not only make me physically fit, but also spiritually fit? How are you challenging yourself to become both physically and spiritually fit?

DAY 28:
Listen for God's Voice

When you pass through the waters, I will be with you; and when you pass through the rivers, they will not sweep over you. (Isaiah 43:2a NIV)

Recently I found myself in a bit of a precarious situation. I decided to go out for an evening paddle despite some cloudiness. All day the skies had vacillated from sunny to cloudy and back to sunny again. It never did rain and the weather report didn't seem to call for rain, so I decided it was safe to go out on the water.

When I first started out, I thought to myself *what a perfect evening for a paddle*! The current was low, and the water was calm; the winds were low, and the clouds shielded me from the blazing sun. Even the bugs were on their best behavior, which is a rare thing in the evenings.

Since the current was low, I decided to go downstream and went about two miles before turning around. Once I did turn around, I could tell the current had increased since I first ventured out.

SUP: SPIRITUAL UNDERSTANDING & PRAYER

About half a mile later around 6 or
6:30pm, the bottom dropped out. The
rain fell so hard there was little visibility.
The water poured into my eyes so I had
to squint my eyes almost fully closed so
my contacts wouldn't get wet or pop out,
making visibility even worse.

Then the winds picked up. While I had
no wind at all going downstream, I now
had a head wind while also having to go
against a stronger current and pelting
rain drops. I had to return to my knees to
lower my center of gravity in the strong
winds and had to paddle with all my
might. Anytime I'd slow down or switch
hands with my paddle, the wind would
try to blow my board back downstream.

There was no one around: not one boat,
not one fisherman. Everyone had taken
cover from the pouring cats and dogs,

but there was no place for me to go. I just had to paddle the remaining mile and a half back upstream.

I have to admit, I was getting nervous and a bit scared. All I could do was pray, "Lord, please just get me back to the harbor." Fortunately, there was no lightning or hail, and despite the winds the water was still pretty calm. I was so thankful for that.

I finally made it back to the docks, but my legs felt like Jell-O. Having to paddle that far on my knees made my leg muscles very shaky. Shivering from the wind blowing on my drenched skin, I was just thankful to finally be back safe and sound.

Two days before this experience, I'd written something down in my journal.

Now, you must understand that, when I journal, I don't record my own thoughts, and I don't write in first person. Instead I record the thoughts God shares with me and write it in His voice. I began this method of journaling several years ago. It takes a lot of quiet time and focus to hear the still, small voice of God, but oh how powerful when you recognize it!

Going back and reading what God was saying is even more powerful. It shows how God knew what He was saying and knew what was going to happen. And, even more important, it shows how God keeps His promises.

Two days before my frightening experience out on the river, God spoke to me through the scripture verse Isaiah 43:2, and I wrote it down in my journal as if He were saying it to me directly: "When you pass through the waters, I will be with you; and when you pass through the rivers, they will not sweep over you." I was so amazed and comforted by this. God knew where I would be two days from then, and He kept His promise to keep me safe.

If you've never spent time trying to hear from God, I encourage you to do so. God starts off by speaking to us softly with a still, small voice, so you have to get quiet to hear Him. Turn off the gadgets, get off social media, and get to a quiet place every day to listen for His voice. Start with reading your Bible because that's one of the first places He'll speak to you. Pay attention to the well-meaning people in your life because He speaks through them as well. You'll be amazed at the difference in your life when you begin to develop these simple yet powerful daily habits.

> *My son, if you receive my words and treasure up my commandments with you, making your ear attentive to wisdom and inclining your heart to understanding; yes, if you call out for insight and raise your voice for understanding, if you seek it like silver and search for it as for hidden treasures, then you will understand the fear of the Lord and find the knowledge of God.*
> *(Proverbs 2:1-5 ESV)*

> *And if you faithfully obey the voice of the Lord your God, being careful to do all his commandments that I command you today, the Lord your God will set you high above all the nations of the earth. And all these blessings shall come upon you and overtake you, if you obey*

the voice of the Lord your God...Give ear, O heavens, and I will speak, and let the earth hear the words of my mouth. May my teaching drop as the rain, my speech distill as the dew, like gentle rain upon the tender grass, and like showers upon the herb.

(Deuteronomy 28:1-2; 32:1-2 ESV)

DAY 29:

Is Your Heart Properly Equipped?

Truly, truly, I say to you, he who hears My word, and believes Him who sent Me, has eternal life.
(John 5:24a NASB)

This past summer, I got to go paddle boarding at Watts Bar Lake in East Tennessee. I was visiting my uncle, and it was his first time paddle boarding. The paddle board he'd borrowed from a friend was missing its fin, and my spare fin didn't fit the fin box of his board, so we had to make do without one.

I let him use my board so he could have one that was properly outfitted, while I tried to manage with the board that had no fin. It's amazing the difference an experience can be when you're not properly equipped versus when you are.

The purpose of a fin is to make the board go straight and keep it stable. I quickly found out what it was like to try and paddle without this important element: my board wanted to go in every direction except straight! Add to that the wind we were experiencing, and I was just being blown around in circles unable to control the board at all. It felt like when you're in a bumper car and you start spinning around. No matter what you do to try to stop spinning, nothing works. I wasn't able to get to where I was trying to go, and if I did, it took A LOT longer without the fin.

That's what our spiritual life can be like when the Holy Spirit is not living inside of us. We aren't properly equipped to remain on a straight path. We'll go in every direction, jumping from one new "self-help" gimmick to the next, oftentimes finding ourselves wasting time just going around in circles with no real results. And we can't stop spinning in circles in our own strength. We need the Holy Spirit to stabilize us.

Therefore, there is now no condemnation for those who are in Christ Jesus, because through Christ Jesus the law of the Spirit who gives life has set you free from the law of sin and death. For what the law was powerless to do because it was weakened by the flesh, God did by sending his own Son in the likeness of sinful flesh to be a sin offering. And so he condemned sin in the flesh, in order that the righteous requirement of the law might be fully met in us, who do not live according to the flesh but according to the Spirit...In the same way the Spirit also helps our weakness; for we do not know how to pray as we should, but the Spirit Himself intercedes for us with groanings too deep for words; and He who searches the hearts knows what the mind of the Spirit is, because He intercedes for the saints according to the will of God. And we know that in all

things God works for the good of those
who love him, who have been called
according to his purpose.
(Romans 8:1-4; 26-28 NIV)

How do you get the Holy Spirit inside you? It's pretty simple. You just admit your need for Him and accept the invitation He's already extended to you, and in turn invite Him into your heart. He does the rest. And you can find security in that, trusting He will direct you on a path that is straight and stable.

DAY 30:

Beware of Making Sharp Turns on Your Spiritual Path

Do not turn to the right or the left;
keep your foot from evil.
(Proverbs 4:27 NIV)

The day after paddling with my uncle at Watts Bar Lake, we headed to downtown Knoxville to try out the hydro bikes at the local paddle shop. Hydro bikes are something I've never done before, so I was very excited to try something new on the water.

These contraptions look like actual bikes from the pedals up, but instead of wheels they have a similar feature on the left and the right as do the amphibious airplanes that land on water. This is what keeps them stable and afloat in the water. In the front where the front wheel would be on a land bike is a front rudder. The handle bars are what turn the rudder so you can control the direction of the bike.

The guy who was working at the paddle shop told us not to turn the handle bars sharper than 45 degrees or else the rudder would be turned sideways, and we'd just be wasting energy pedaling and getting nowhere (much like if you turn the handlebars too sharp on a regular bike).

Just like in our spiritual walk, if we turn too sharp to the left or too sharp to the right, we can get stuck or stalled in our spiritual journey. Yes we will experience a few curves in our path, but we mustn't overcorrect. We must make the adjustments in our steering that are within our control, and trust God to do the rest to get us straight and back on the path.

Failure is a part of life, and there will always be times when we as humans will fail. But God's promises do not.

"Be strong and courageous. Do not be afraid or terrified because of them, for

the Lord your God goes with you; he
will never leave you nor forsake you."
Then Moses summoned Joshua and
said to him in the presence of all Isra-
el, "Be strong and courageous, for you
must go with this people into the land
that the Lord swore to their ancestors
to give them, and you must divide it
among them as their inheritance. The
Lord himself goes before you and will
be with you; he will never leave you nor
forsake you. Do not be afraid; do not be
discouraged."
(Deuteronomy 31:6-8 NIV)

God is always available to help us
straighten out our lives and start over.
When we acknowledge our sins, He is
ready and willing to help us start again.

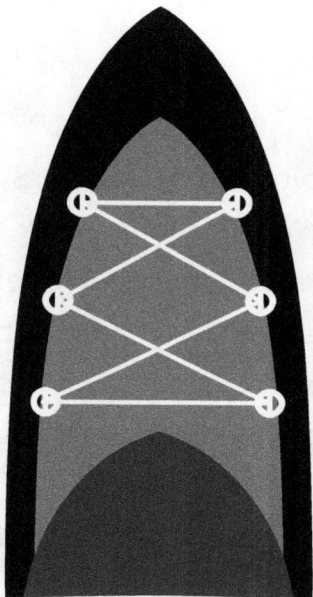

CONCLUSION

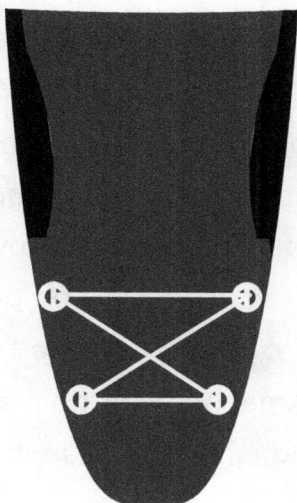

CONCLUSION

The idea to turn some of my SUP blog
entries into a devotional book came at
the encouragement of my publisher,
Hilliard Press. Hilliard Press published
my first book, the Amazon #1 bestselling
book *Advance Your Image*, and wanted
a second book from me. As an answer to
their request, I originally thought about
doing an instructional book on how to
discover your passions and find work you
love, but the Holy Spirit led me in a different direction.

When I presented the idea of a devotional book instead, they loved it. Only after
I started compiling my blog entries did it
dawn on me I could use the money from
the book sales to help fund my very first
mission trip. In 2017, I will be going with
my church to Brazil. We'll be traveling
down the Amazon River on a small boat
and sleeping in hammocks while making

stops at small communities along the river helping with everything from construction and home visits to ministry at local churches.

I want to thank you for your purchase of this book, and want you to know that, because of this purchase, you're making a difference in the lives of so many people. If you'd like to purchase an additional copy for a friend or family member, please contact me directly at lorib@yourpassioninlife.com. Proceeds will go to Justice and Mercy Amazon.

To read additional blog entries from *Spiritual Understanding & Prayer on a SUP*, go to http://supspirituallessons.blogspot.com

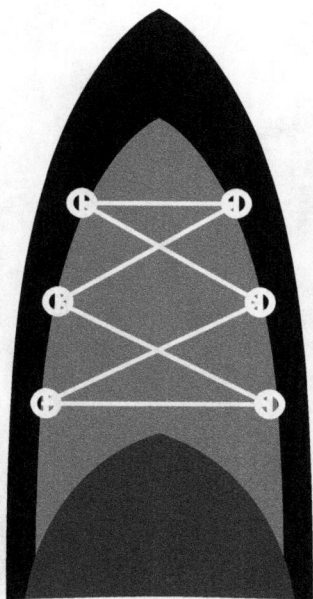

ABOUT THE AUTHOR

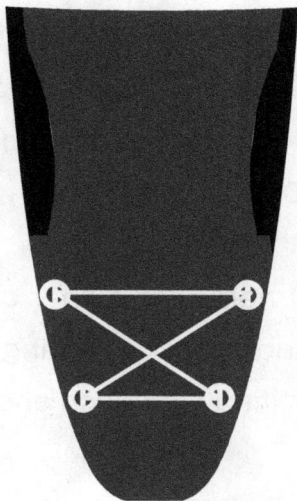

"I believe you can find the courage to discover and pursue your passions despite the obstacles you may face. I want to see you actively pursue your passions with flair ('paNASH') and confidence, along with responsibility to your purpose in life." Lori Bumgarner, Passion & Career Specialist/Owner of paNASH

Lori Bumgarner is the owner of paNASH, a passion and career coaching service, and is a certified life coach and certified

transformational coach. After completing her master's degree in education, she worked for ten years as a college career adviser at various universities including Vanderbilt University and Belmont University in Nashville, Tennessee, where she now calls home. She loved her work as a career adviser, but was ready for a new challenge and environment.

With a desire to do something different, Lori left her full-time job with benefits to start her own image consulting and media coaching business in the music industry…right before the economy tanked in 2008. "Most people would have considered the recession bad timing when just starting a business, but I admit that if the recession had occurred before I left my job, I would have been too afraid to pursue a passion that allowed me to use my creativity."

SUP: SPIRITUAL UNDERSTANDING & PRAYER

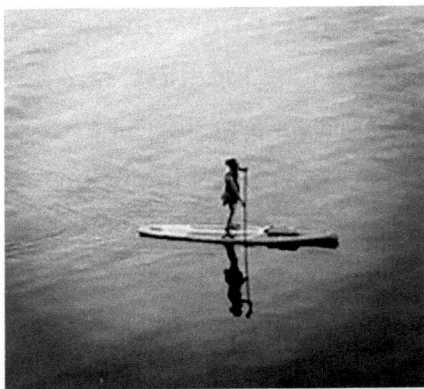

After eight years of working with up-and-coming recording artists, it was time for Lori to teach and coach others on how to push through their fears and pursue their own passions. She completed her coaching certification and changed her business's focus and mission which became "to serve, educate, and encourage others by assisting them with the discovery and pursuit of their passions in a way that honors their purpose and their own vision for success, while amplifying who they are personally and advancing them professionally."

Lori's previous publications include the Amazon #1 bestselling book *Advance Your Image*, and she has been featured in *The Wall Street Journal's* blog, *The Daily Positive*, Arianna Huffington's *Thrive Global,* and *The Huffington Post and Inc*. Lori is passionate about God, stand up paddling, exploring new interests, life-long learning, and encouraging others. Her personal mission is to boldly pursue her passions and purpose, and to teach, encourage, and inspire others to do the same, resulting in lives overflowing with joy, peace, and fulfillment.

You can visit Lori's web site at www.yourpassioninlife.com or email her directly at lorib@yourpassioninlife.com.